ANIMALS HIBERNATING

HOW ANIMALS SURVIVE EXTREME CONDITIONS

WRITTEN BY PAMELA HICKMAN

ILLUSTRATED BY PAT STEPHENS

Kids Can Press

It takes many people to produce a book and I'd like to acknowledge the hard work and great talent of illustrator, Pat Stephens, designer, Marie Bartholomew and editor Stacey Roderick. Thankfully, the staff at Kids Can Press don't hibernate!

For Jasmine — PH
For my mother — PS

Text © 2005 Pamela Hickman
Illustrations © 2005 Pat Stephens

Neither the Publisher nor the Author shall be liable for any damage that may be caused or sustained as a result of conducting any of the activities in this book without specifically following instructions, conducting the activities without proper supervision or ignoring the cautions contained in the book.

Kids Can Press acknowledges the financial support of the Government of Ontario, through the Ontario Media Development Corporation's Ontario Book Initiative; the Ontario Arts Council; the Canada Council for the Arts; and the Government of Canada, through the BPIDP, for our publishing activity.

Published in Canada by
Kids Can Press Ltd.
29 Birch Avenue
Toronto, ON M4V 1E2

Published in the U.S. by
Kids Can Press Ltd.
2250 Military Road
Tonawanda, NY 14150

www.kidscanpress.com

Edited by Stacey Roderick
Designed by Marie Bartholomew
Printed and bound in China

The hardcover edition of this book is smyth sewn casebound.
The paperback edition of this book is limp sewn with a drawn-on cover.

CM 05 0 9 8 7 6 5 4 3 2 1
CM PA 05 0 9 8 7 6 5 4 3 2 1

Library and Archives Canada Cataloguing in Publication

Hickman, Pamela
   Animals hibernating : how animals survive extreme conditions / written by Pamela Hickman ; illustrated by Pat Stephens.

Includes index.

ISBN 1-55337-662-5 (bound). ISBN 1-55337-663-3 (pbk.)

1. Hibernation —Juvenile literature. I. Title.

QL755.H43 2005   j591.56'5   C2005-901176-9

Kids Can Press is a CORUS™ Entertainment company

Contents

Introduction

Imagine going to sleep in July and waking up in April, like a hibernating Belding ground squirrel! Or what if you spent the winter frozen almost solid like a baby painted turtle? These are just a couple of examples of the hidden world of hibernating animals.

Instead of using up lots of energy trying to stay warm and find food during winter's extreme cold, many species simply find shelter and become inactive, or dormant. This is called hibernation. Hibernators are divided into two groups: true hibernators and deep sleepers.

True hibernators, such as chipmunks, save energy during winter by greatly lowering their body temperature and breathing and heart rates. True hibernators also include creatures such as

insects, toads and snakes, whose bodies partly freeze and then thaw again in the spring.

Instead of a true hibernation, other animals, such as skunks and raccoons, go into a deep sleep for several weeks or months during winter. Their breathing and heart rates drop, but their body temperature lowers only slightly.

In this book you'll meet all kinds of extreme sleepers, from bats that hang together in groups of hundreds or more to woodchucks that curl up in a ball alone. You'll also find out how your heart rate compares with a hibernating bat's, why maple syrup is like a hibernating frog's blood, and much more.

See you in the spring

Many animals deal with cold temperatures and lack of food in winter by finding a sheltered spot and staying there until spring. True hibernators, such as hedgehogs, are inactive much longer than deep sleepers, such as fox squirrels. True hibernators shut down their body functions until they are barely alive. This extreme state is called torpor.

Some true hibernators, such as insects, frogs and turtles, can stay active only as long as the air is warm. Once the cool weather arrives, they have to hibernate to survive. Not only do they become inactive, but some also freeze nearly solid during winter!

This Arctic ground squirrel, the largest and most northern ground squirrel in North America, is a true hibernator. It is the only known mammal that can survive dropping its body temperature to –2 to –3°C (28 to 27°F). People can't survive a body temperature below 32°C (90°F).

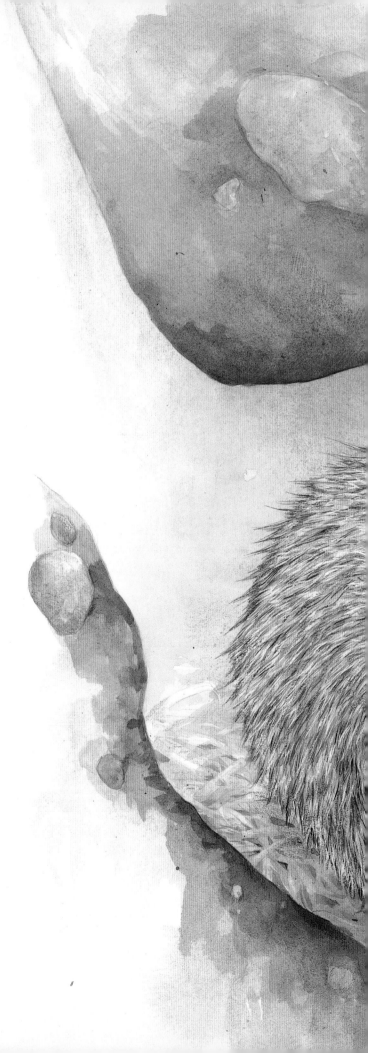

If you were an Arctic ground squirrel ...

- you would dig a special hibernation chamber, or room, off your main burrow, about 0.5 m (20 in.) deep.
- in late summer, you would line the chamber with grass, lichen, leaves and animal hair for warmth and comfort. You would store food such as seeds.
- you would roll up into a ball and cover your head and shoulders with your furry tail.
- you would enter a state of torpor but wake briefly every few weeks during your seven-month hibernation.

Who hibernates and why?

Have you ever thought it would be nice to go to sleep and wake up when all your worries are gone? Hibernation is a bit like that. Animals hibernate to avoid life-threatening conditions, including extremely cold temperatures and lack of food or water.

Mammals and birds are endotherms, commonly called warm-blooded animals. Food supply is their biggest problem in winter. Endotherms control their body temperature and keep it at a constant, high level. This requires a lot of energy from food. In winter, it is impossible for some endotherms to find enough food to eat to stay warm. By lowering their body temperature, hibernating endotherms use less energy and need less food.

True hibernation is more common in smaller endotherms than larger ones. Meadow jumping mice, for example, lose body heat fast and need more energy to stay warm than foxes, which don't hibernate.

Insects, frogs and snakes are examples of ectotherms, also known as cold-blooded animals. Cold weather is their biggest challenge. Ectotherms rely on the outside weather to warm up or cool down. As the temperature drops in autumn, ectotherms get colder and their bodies slow down. They must find shelter and hibernate before they can't function at all and die. Most ectotherms are true hibernators, and they become active again only when warm weather returns.

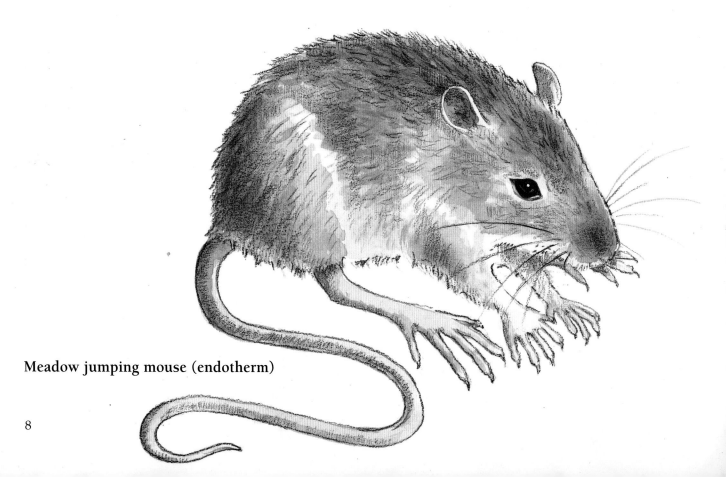

Meadow jumping mouse (endotherm)

8

Hibernating bird discovered?

On December 28, 1946, Dr. Edmund Jaeger believed he had found the first hibernating bird. The common poorwill he found in the mountains of southern California had extremely slow breathing and heart rates, and its body temperature was far below normal. Recent studies by Canadian biologist Dr. Chris Woods found poorwills in Arizona inactive for up to ten weeks at a time. Unlike true hibernators, though, the poorwills' body temperature rose and fell dramatically from day to day. More study is needed to decide whether these birds can be considered true hibernators.

Common poorwill

Smooth green snake (ectotherm)

Barely alive

Did you know your body temperature and breathing rate drop slightly when you sleep? This helps your body save energy. True hibernating endotherms go to an even greater extreme. Hoary marmots, woodchucks and other true hibernators enter a state of torpor off and on during the several months they hibernate.

An animal in torpor feels cold and looks dead. Its body temperature drops to a few degrees above freezing or even colder. Its heart rate and breathing slow dramatically. Some animals will stop breathing entirely for short periods of time.

While animals are in this unconscious state of torpor, they don't eat or drink. Instead, their bodies gradually use up their stored fat. Mouse lemurs hibernate up to seven months, surviving only on their fat.

Torpor lasts from a few days at a time to several weeks. It is usually shortest during the beginning and end of true hibernation and longest during mid-winter. Between periods of torpor, true hibernators wake briefly to warm up inside their shelter.

Hoary marmot

Mouse lemur

How do you rate?

A little brown bat's heart normally beats 400–700 times per minute during activity, but only 7–10 times per minute in hibernation. With the help of a friend, find out how you compare.

You'll need:

a skipping rope

a clock with a second hand

a pencil and notepad

1. Jump rope or run on the spot for three minutes.

2. Have a friend place her index and middle fingers on your pulse (on your wrist, just below your thumb) and count how many times your heart beats in 60 seconds. This is your heart rate. At the same time, count how many breaths you take. Record both numbers.

3. Sit down and relax for ten minutes. Then measure your heart rate and breathing rate again. Compare them to your first records.

4. Switch places, and test your friend.

You should find that your heart and breathing rates are highest after exercising. The higher the numbers, the more energy your body is using. During hibernation, a bat's body slows down so that it uses very little energy.

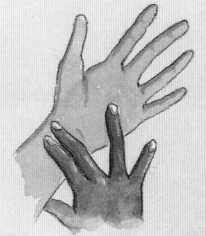

Freezing cold

Wood frog

In science fiction movies, people who have been frozen for years can come back to life. People can't really survive freezing like that, but several kinds of frogs, turtles, fish, insects and other ectotherms can. They freeze nearly solid during hibernation and wake up again in the spring.

Wood frogs bury themselves in the ground in fall. As the temperature drops, the frogs gradually freeze, beginning with their hind legs and ending with their vital organs: their heart and brain.

Why doesn't freezing kill them? Their liver produces a special type of sugar called glucose. Acting like a natural antifreeze, the glucose travels through their bodies in their blood and prevents long-term damage to their cells.

Painted turtle hatchlings, or babies, can survive temperatures as low as −4°C (25°F). Over half of their body water turns to ice, their heart stops and their blood stops flowing. They can live like this for up to five months!

Southern painted turtle hatchlings

Sweet solution

Before you pour maple syrup on your pancakes, use it for this activity. Maple syrup is a highly concentrated, sugary liquid similar to the glucose-rich blood of hibernating frogs and turtles.

You'll need:

2 250 mL (8 oz.) plastic containers with lids, such as yogurt containers

water

pure maple syrup

a freezer

1. Pour water into one container, leaving a 2.5 cm (1 in.) space at the top. Put the lid on tightly.

2. Fill the other container with an equal amount of maple syrup and put the lid on.

3. Place both containers in the freezer overnight.

4. Check the containers.

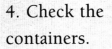

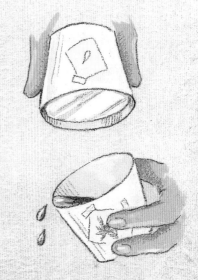

You should find that the container full of water is frozen solid and the maple syrup is still liquid. The high concentration of sugar in the syrup keeps it from freezing solid, just as glucose prevents the blood of hibernating ectotherms from freezing solid.

Getting ready

Autumn is a busy time for hibernators. First they choose a warm and safe space for hibernating, called a hibernaculum. Then their thoughts turn to food.

Dormice are true hibernators that gather food and store it inside their winter chamber. When they waken briefly between periods of torpor, they snack on their seeds and nuts. Other true hibernators, such as meadow jumping mice, don't eat or drink during hibernation, so they eat as much food as possible beforehand in the fall. All that eating adds a thick layer of fat to their bodies for warmth and energy. Most deep sleepers, such as bears and raccoons, also fatten up before heading to their beds.

Raccoons curl up with their families, but this woodchuck, also called a groundhog, is a true hibernator that prefers to be alone in its hibernaculum.

If you were a woodchuck ...

- you would start gaining a thick layer of fat in late summer.
- you would dig a special burrow deep underground, and you would use soil to block yourself in by the end of October.
- you would roll yourself into a ball and tuck your head between your hind legs.
- your body temperature would lower to 2–3°C (35–37°F), and your breathing rate would drop as low as one breath every five minutes.
- you would lose about one-third of your weight during your six-month hibernation.

Digging in

Choosing the right place to hibernate can mean the difference between life and death.

During hibernation, animals are easy prey. The harder it is for predators to find or dig out a hibernating animal, the safer that animal is.

Digging deeply also helps animals stay warm. Burrowers usually dig their chambers so they will be below the frozen ground, where it is warmer. Once sealed shut, these chambers stay above freezing temperature and are humid, or moist.

Humidity makes breathing easier and keeps the animals healthier.

Many animals line their burrows or dens with leaves, grasses, twigs or animal hair to make them warmer and more comfortable. Polar bears, which are deep sleepers, dig dens into snowbanks or snowdrifts. The snow acts like a warm blanket to protect the bears from the cold. Other animals bed down in caves, hollow trees or underwater mud. Can you match the animals below with their winter hideouts?

3. Whitetail prairie dogs

1. Eastern pipistrelle bats

2. Raccoons

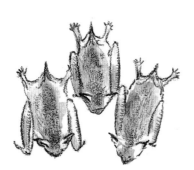

4. American badger

5. Snapping turtle

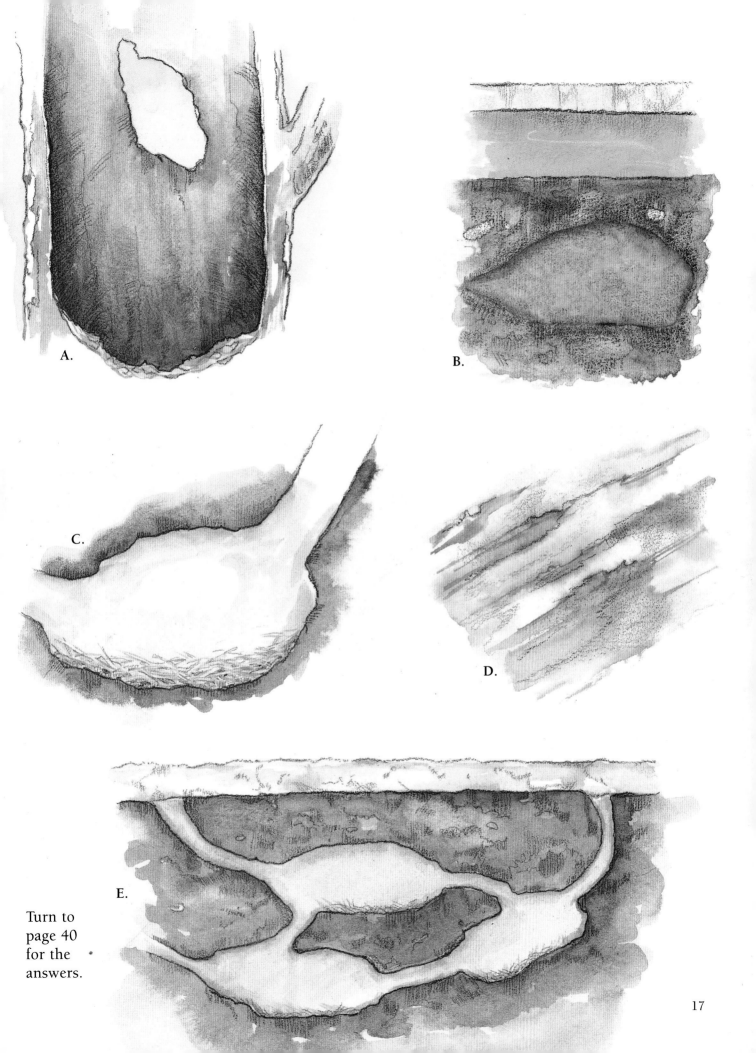

A.

B.

C.

D.

E.

Turn to page 40 for the answers.

Getting together

Cuddling with your furry mother, brothers and sisters is a great way to stay warm during a cold winter. Groups of up to twelve skunks, usually females and their young, gather together. Female raccoons and bears also sleep in family groups. Mothers help keep their babies warm and protect them from danger at the same time.

Skunks

More body heat is just one advantage of hibernating in a group. In some areas, there may be only a few safe spots for hibernating. By sharing the space, more animals survive the winter. Big brown bats gather in large caves and may hang in clusters of over 100 bats! Thousands of garter snakes hibernate together in a heap in rocky crevices.

Finding a mate is also much easier when everyone winters together. Little brown bats may mate in the fall, when they gather together in groups of hundreds or thousands in their hibernaculum. During mild spells, the bats become active and mate again inside their cave. Yellow-bellied marmots hibernate in colonies, or large groups, in the central Rocky Mountains. They mate when they come out of hibernation.

Big brown bats

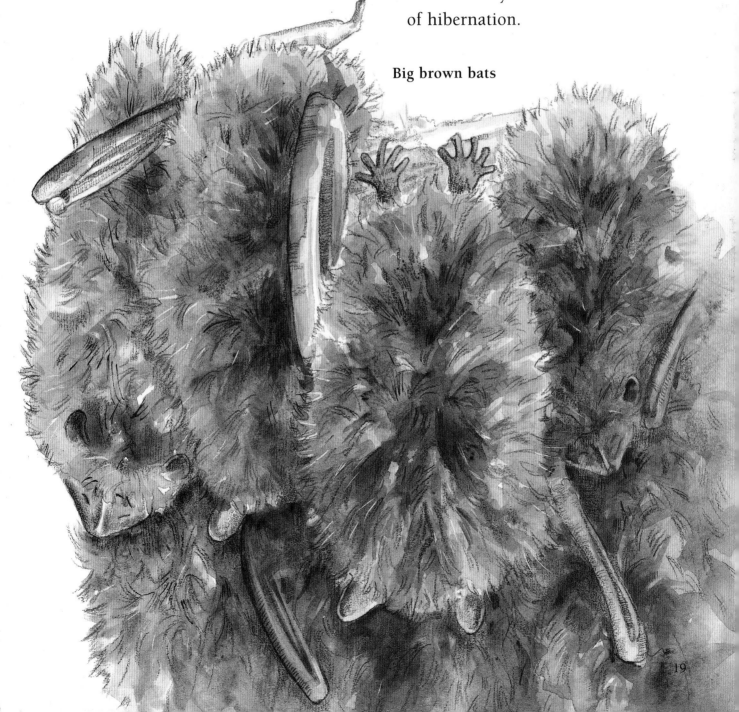

Fall feast

Putting on lots of fat in a short time is considered unhealthy for people, but it saves the lives of many hibernators. Without a thick layer of stored fat, some hibernating animals would not survive the winter.

During hibernation, fat is slowly absorbed by an animal's body. Fat supplies water, food and enough energy to support the animal's low body temperature and slow heart and breathing rates. Most animals lose up to half their body fat during hibernation. And since they are barely functioning, hibernating animals don't grow — that would require too much energy.

Fat also keeps the animal warmer. This is why the European hedgehog eats so much in the fall. Baby toads will double their size before digging in for the winter. And black bears gain up to 13.5 kg (30 lb.) a week when they are preparing for their deep sleep.

When animals gain a lot of extra fat, it makes them sleepy and less energetic. And as food becomes harder to find, it takes more energy to gather. Eventually, the animal is too tired to look for more food and enters its hibernaculum. Young animals take longer than adults to build up their stored fat, so they begin their hibernation later.

European hedgehog

The amount of stored fat affects other body functions. Female black bears give birth during their deep sleep. Growing the babies inside of them and nursing them once they are born requires a lot of energy. Bears that don't gain enough fat before going to sleep may not produce young.

Instead of storing food as body fat, eastern chipmunks use their large cheek pouches to carry food back to their burrows for snacking during the winter. Up to 8 L (2 gal.) of seeds and nuts have been found in a chipmunk's burrow. That's many times larger than the chipmunk!

Columbian ground squirrels not only eat a lot in the fall but also gather seeds and bulbs to store in their hibernation chamber to eat after waking in the spring.

Eastern chipmunk

Columbian ground squirrel

The inside story

Most true hibernators briefly wake up many times throughout the winter and may even eat and go to the bathroom before entering torpor again. It takes several hours for them to wake up. But a deep sleeper, like this black bear, takes only a few minutes to awaken. It is inactive, or dormant, during extremely cold conditions, but may wake during mild weather. One advantage of being a deep sleeper is that the bear can become aware of danger and protect itself much faster than a true hibernator.

If you were a black bear ...

- you would find winter shelter in a cave, hollow log or upturned stump.
- you would put on a thick layer of fat and grow extra fur in the fall to keep you warm.
- you would not eat, drink or go to the bathroom for several months while hibernating.
- your body temperature would drop only a few degrees, but your breathing and heart rate would be much lower than normal.
- you would be easily disturbed by noise.

Sleep walkers and eaters

Mourning cloak butterfly

Deep sleepers may wake up on warmer winter days. Male skunks wander around outside on mild days. Hibernating water insects, such as backswimmers, may leave their muddy burrows and swim to the surface. Adult mourning cloak butterflies fly around on warm, sunny winter days but return to their bark shelter before sundown. Flying squirrels, black-tailed prairie dogs and opossum seek shelter during stormy winter weather but reappear when it clears up.

A true hibernator may wake from extreme cold. If it is in danger of freezing to death, an animal may wake to warm up slightly.

Scientists believe that when animals wake during hibernation, their bodies may make slight adjustments that keep the animals healthy. It's a bit like tuning up a bike or car. Chipmunks and some other true hibernators eat and go to the bathroom during their few hours awake between periods of torpor.

Sleep watching

Scientists have developed tiny radio transmitters they attach to animals before they burrow for the winter. The transmitters help them monitor the animals' body temperature, heart and breathing rates, and movement.

Flying squirrel

Towel trick

Try this simple experiment to see why woodchucks and other mammals roll up into a tight ball inside their hibernation chamber.

You'll need:

2 similar towels

a clothes dryer

2 clothespins

a coathanger

1. Put the towels into a hot dryer for five minutes.

2. Fold one towel in half and then in half again. Then roll it up like a bedroll (see illustration).

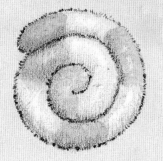

3. Hang the other towel from the hanger using the clothespins.

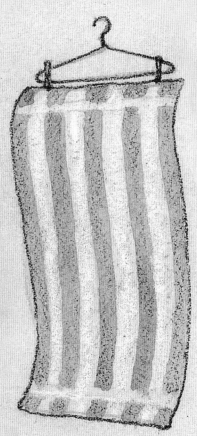

4. After five minutes, feel the hanging towel. Unroll the other towel and feel it. Which is warmer?

You should find that the rolled-up towel stayed warmer. That's because less of its surface area was exposed to the cooling air. Similarly, mammals curl up into a tight ball during hibernation. Since less of the animals' surface area, or skin, is exposed to the cold air, they stay warmer longer.

Hibernating hazards

A long, cold, snowy winter may mean lots of skiing and snowboarding fun for you, but it can mean death for some hibernating animals.

The main challenge is to have enough food. As long as hibernating animals store plenty of food or put on enough fat in the fall, they can stay hidden away until warmer weather arrives. But if winter is longer than normal, they could run out of food and starve.

Little brown bats die if they don't store enough body fat to last them the six or seven months they spend hibernating. A long winter also delays the hatching and waking of insects the bats eat.

Extreme temperatures and predators are other hibernating hazards. Even the best hibernaculum may not keep an animal from freezing to death. This is especially true in the Arctic, where animals can dig only shallow burrows in the permanently frozen ground. And sometimes predators find and dig out hibernating animals. A combination of cold, predators and lack of food kills almost half of hibernating adult chipmunks and even more young ones. And up to 93 percent of young Belding ground squirrels die during hibernation for the same reasons.

Pollution and the destruction of fields, forests and marshes can destroy the winter habitats of various animals so they have no place to hibernate. Occasionally, construction workers dig up hibernating animals by accident. One of the first times the inside of a woodchuck's winter home was seen happened when a bulldozer toppled the tree the animal was hibernating under.

Weasels, foxes and wolves are
experts at finding hidden prey.

Rise and shine

How does a hibernating animal know when it is time to wake up? As spring approaches, the animal starts to spend more time awake. Eventually, the temperature is warm enough to signal the end of hibernation. You might think the animals would be in a hurry to see the sun again, but not all hibernators come out of their shelters right away.

Ectotherms, such as insects, reptiles and these salamanders, can't get moving until they have warmed up enough. During the first cool days of spring in the northern part of their range, these animals are still very sluggish.

If you were a male spotted salamander ...

- you would hibernate in a burrow under a rock or rotting log.
- you would rely on the warmer spring temperatures to wake you up.
- you would come out of your burrow at night during the first warm rains in March or early April.
- you would awaken a few days before the females and wait for them at a breeding pond. You would mate when the females arrived.

When do they wake up?

You might see a skunk on a mild February day in Canada, but you wouldn't see a skink until the spring. The Belding ground squirrel hibernates longer than any other North American mammal: eight months a year! Turkish hamsters in the Middle East can hibernate for ten continuous months. Big brown bats are among the first bats to appear in spring—after as little as four months in their cave. How long animals hibernate depends on a number of factors, including weather, where the animal lives and the species.

The longer the cold weather lasts, the longer the hibernation. Hibernators stay put until the outside temperatures are warm enough to keep the air and soil constantly above freezing.

The same kind of animal will hibernate for different lengths of time depending on where it lives. For example, American badgers living in colder northern areas hibernate for up to six months. Those living farther south may spend just a couple of weeks dormant, and only during severe winter weather.

In many species, the males become active first. Male Richardson's ground squirrels spend a week eating their stored food before leaving the den to battle other males for mates. The females emerge about two weeks later, after waking up only the day before.

Pregnant female polar bears stay in their den for 160 to 170 days waiting for spring, but males find shelter only during bad weather. They are out hunting most of the winter.

Five-lined skink

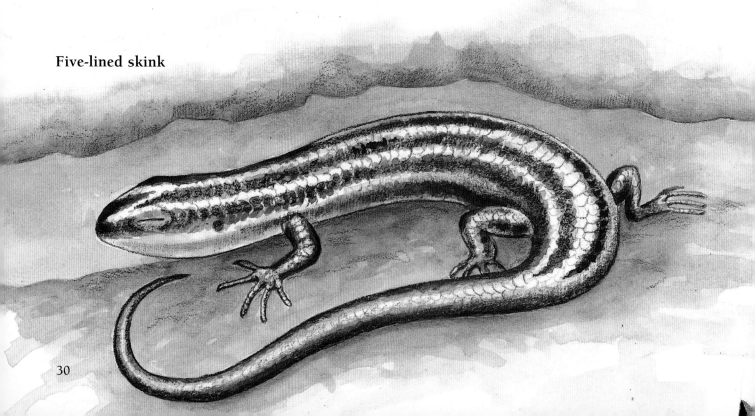

Turkish hamster

Polar bears

Groundhog day

Wiarton Willie, Shubenacadie Sam and Punxsutawney Phil are the most famous groundhogs, or woodchucks, in North America. Every February 2, thousands of people gather to see whether the emerging groundhogs will see their shadows. An old German legend says that if a groundhog sees its shadow, there will be six more weeks of winter. If not, spring is just around the corner. The truth is that groundhogs can't predict the weather any better than you!

Wiarton Willie is albino, or all white, unlike most groundhogs.

Thawing out

Are you a morning person? Some people are slow and grouchy in the morning, even after a good night's sleep. Just imagine what they'd be like after sleeping for six months or so!

Deep sleepers don't lower their body temperatures much during dormancy, so waking and warming up may take only a few minutes, even for large animals. But waking up from true hibernation is a big adjustment for an animal's body.

One of the first things to happen is a gradual rise in body temperature. As well as the extra fat they put on for the winter, some mammals have a special kind of fat called brown fat. When absorbed by the body, its energy quickly produces heat to help the animal warm up.

Other mammals shiver violently to generate body heat. Slowly their body temperature returns to normal, beginning with the heart and brain tissues and ending with the ears, feet and tail. As their body temperature rises, their heart and breathing rates increase.

Ectotherms, such as reptiles and insects, cannot warm themselves. They have to wait until warm weather raises their body temperature. As frozen frogs and turtles thaw out, their heart, the last organ to freeze, is the first to warm up and start working again.

An animal's size can affect how quickly it warms up. The body temperature of small true hibernators, such as dormice, can rise ten times faster than that of larger animals such as badgers.

Once warm, an animal's troubles may not be over. For example, a study of chipmunks showed that the animals suffered from temporary brain damage, memory loss and confusion as they warmed up and became active again. They soon returned to normal, though.

Dormouse

Leopard frog

Cool research

Medical researchers are trying to figure out what combination of chemicals allows frogs and turtles to survive freezing with no cell damage. If scientists can solve the puzzle, they may be able to use the same chemicals to preserve human organs, such as hearts and lungs, longer for transplant. Or they could possibly preserve a human body in a frozen-like state while it is waiting for a transplant! Now that's cool!

Active again

If you were out of action for several months, what would you do first when you woke up? Different animals do different things when they come out of hibernation, including drink, eat and mate.

Mammals that don't store food are hungry and thirsty when they emerge. Big brown bats head for water to drink, and woodchucks search for a snack. Since there is often snow on the ground when woodchucks emerge, their usual diet of green plants hasn't grown yet. They have to eat bark and twigs until the tender greens sprout again.

Animals like Arctic ground squirrels are more prepared. They store seeds and leaves in their burrows for the spring. That way they have food while they are waiting for new plants to grow.

Male toads, frogs and other amphibians head straight to breeding ponds, where they wait for the females to join them. A sure sign of the end of hibernation is the chorus of spring peepers calling for mates from ponds and marshes. Chipmunks also mate soon after leaving their burrows, while many species of bats mate just before leaving their caves. Badgers mate before hibernation, and the females give birth shortly after they emerge. Bears have their cubs during dormancy.

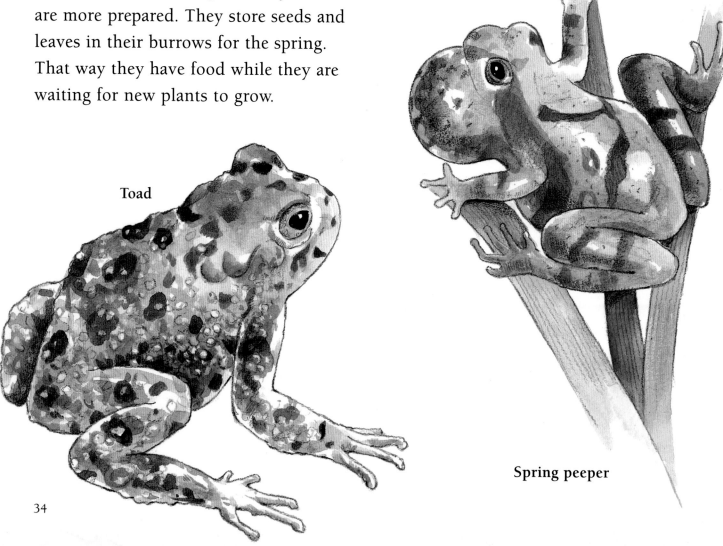

Toad

Spring peeper

Insects can spend winter in various stages of their life cycle. For example, different butterflies hibernate at different stages in their development. Hibernation may happen at the egg, caterpillar, chrysalis or adult stage. Once the weather warms up, the eggs hatch and other life stages gradually continue to develop into adults. Early-awakening insects are food for many insect-eating hibernators that have also just woken up.

Tiger swallowtail butterfly

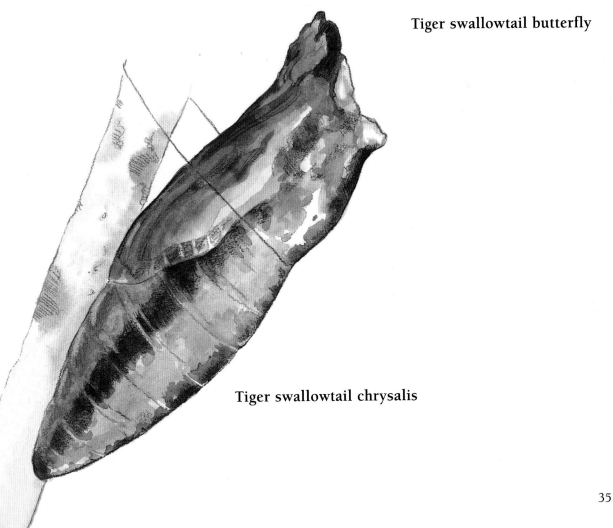

Tiger swallowtail chrysalis

Other extreme sleepers

In addition to hibernation, there are two other ways that animals shut down their bodies to survive: daily torpor and aestivation.

Some animals need to save energy all year round, so they enter a brief state of torpor every day. By slowing their bodies down for a few hours per day, shrews, chickadees and other animals get a rest and need less food to survive.

Animals that live in cold climates aren't the only ones that need to avoid extreme weather. Many insects, desert amphibians, tortoises, snails and other creatures live where drought or high temperatures are common. These animals also seek shelter and become inactive for long periods of time. This is called aestivation. Unlike hibernators that try to stay warm, aestivators try to keep as cool as possible.

One of the world's most amazing aestivators is this water-holding frog from the dry interior parts of Australia. It has saved Australian Aboriginal people from dying of thirst in the desert. They dig up the frogs and squeeze out the stored water to drink.

If you were a water-holding frog ...

- you would live most of the year buried in an underground burrow.
- you would fill your large bladder with water before burying yourself.
- you would shed dry skin and produce mucous to create a layered, waterproof lining, like a cocoon, inside your burrow.
- you would slowly absorb the water from your bladder so you didn't dry out.
- you would dig yourself out during heavy rain.

Daily dozers

If you're tired, you might nap during the day. Some mammals and birds do something similar in order to survive! These animals need to eat constantly to have enough energy to stay active. To save energy, they enter a state of torpor for several hours a day. While in their few hours of daily torpor, bats save up to 99 percent of their energy.

During daily torpor, an animal's body temperature and breathing and heart rates lower, but not as dramatically as a hibernating animal's. Shrews, bats, lemurs, hummingbirds, swallows and martins are just some of the creatures that go into daily torpor. Dwarf lemurs of Madagascar are believed to be the only primates (a group of mammals that includes monkeys, apes and humans) that go into daily torpor.

Unlike hibernation, daily torpor does not require any preparation. But it can take up to three hours for an animal to get back to its normal state.

The tawny frogmouth, a large Australian bird, enters torpor twice a day during winter. Since it needs less energy to survive, the species can stay in its territory all year instead of migrating to look for food when temperatures drop.

Chickadees, finches and other small birds don't just go to sleep at night. Their body temperature drops by three to five degrees, and their energy use drops to nearly half of their normal rate. This adaptation helps the birds survive cooler temperatures when they are not eating.

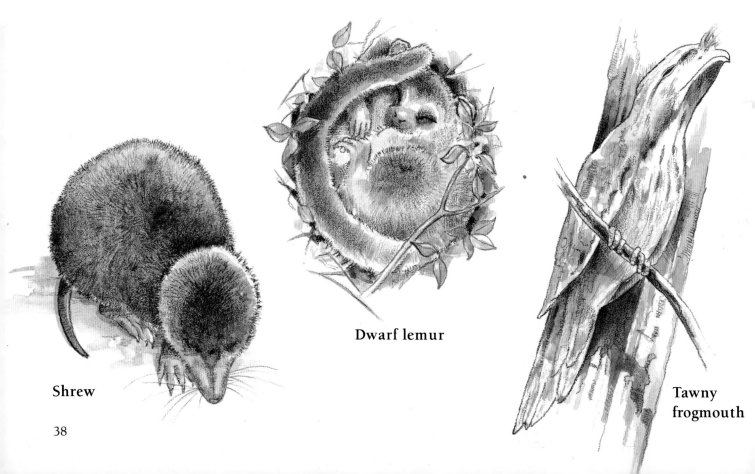

Shrew

Dwarf lemur

Tawny frogmouth

Hummingbird

Swallows

Chickadees

Glossary

aestivation: a dormant state some animals enter to survive very hot or dry weather.

deep sleeper: an animal that is dormant during the coldest part of winter but may wake and be active on mild days. Its breathing and heart rates drop, but its body temperature lowers only slightly.

dormancy: a period of inactivity that usually last days or weeks.

ectotherm: an animal that relies on the outside temperature to raise or lower its body temperature. Ectotherms are sometimes called cold-blooded.

endotherm: an animal that controls its own body temperature, keeping it at a constant, high level. Endotherms are sometimes called warm-blooded.

hibernation: a sleep-like state that some animals enter to survive winter.

torpor: a deep state of dormancy, experienced by true hibernators, lasting days or weeks. To save energy, some animals enter daily torpor for a few hours every day.

true hibernator: an animal that drastically lowers its body temperature and breathing and heart rates during dormancy in winter. Some true hibernators freeze nearly solid and then thaw again in spring.

Index

Answers
Pages 16–17
1-D, 2-A, 3-E, 4-C, 5-B